FLAWED BUT FUN:
Poems from the Attic

with an epilogue on mental illness

Nancy Tuininga

To Kristen ~
With Best wishes!
Nancy Tuininga

Peregrine Images

for Julie, Kristin and Andy,

with love

CONTENTS

FOREWORD

Nancy Tuininga was an extremely bright, energetic, compassionate woman in her mid-twenties when the dark shadow of bipolar disorder first descended upon her. Thus began a heroic 40-year struggle to maintain some semblance of family, career, and intellectual life while under assault from this crippling affliction. The fact that she functions today as a contributing member of society is testimony to her exceptional courage, keen intellect, and sheer determination.

Sustaining Nancy through much of this dark journey has been her writing of poems. Many are precious jewels, a unique combination of incisive insight, poignant humor, and painful truths. However, all are particularly insightful as a window into an especially gifted mind which has been savagely challenged. Her poems have also been her compass to lucidity and a source of self-worth in many of her darkest moments.

Nancy's unusual courage to write objectively and intelligently in the epilogue about her illness is an insightful gift to anyone experiencing similar problems personally or with loved ones. It also serves as a reminder that much of the continuing societal stigma of mental illness is unwarranted.

We take great pleasure in sharing with you the precious, life sustaining work of this very special woman.

Hal Eastman, Publisher

THE POEMS

A Lie-Down

I had a little "cat."
(It wasn't quite a nap.)
Right in the middle of the day.
It straightened out my potpourri of disarray
And brightened up my way.

Aplomb*

Puny notions of aplomb abound.
The highest grace bestowed, without a sound
Is manifested in the chipmunk's dance of glee
As he scampers 'round a little twig of a tree
Showing off for me.
He perches with his tiny paws alert
Then scrambles with the slightest evidence of
         motion
On my part.
His defense is quite plain;
He travels to the back side
Of a larger tree
Quickly, deftly becoming invisible
To me.

*Aplomb: complete and confident composure or
self-assurance: POISE.

Bits and Bytes

Bits and bytes
And unhatched polliwog eggs
Have something in common:
They both grow legs
And try like mad to maintain some congruity
Amidst an atmosphere that begs
The spread of growth,
Developing
Websites that hop all over the place,
Sometimes even into outer space.
Would God approve?

The frog becomes a harmless jumping entity,
Staying in his natural groove
But websites are incessant strivers
Proliferating information to a fare-thee-well
Perhaps, even into hell itself.

Is it all for pelf?*

*Pelf: Money or wealth, esp. when regarded with
contempt or acquired by reprehensible means.

Braking*

I did!
I just asked her
And she said that red cars go faster
So I gave it a sigh
As she started to cry
And I said if the sky
Was the limit on speed
We'd put tears on spears
And use them to water the trees.
She understood,
And said that she would
Slow down
And the next time she drove
Through town
She was wearing a cap and gown.

*A traffic officer is talking. He has just stopped a young woman for speeding. She is driving a red car.

Bunk

I have "imps".
Imaginary so called important thoughts
That overwhelm my imagination
Causing me to think I have bought
Into superlative exaggeration.
Suddenly I realize that the
Entire thought or thought process
May simply just be "bunk".
Or "thought junk".

For example I recently went on a diet;
Started cutting back on my portions,
Found myself abstaining tortuously.
Then I said to myself "bunk"!
And began gorging on pickles, chips,
Ice cream, chocolate, cream cheese
And tons of junk food. Why not?
Americans are famous for being
Fat anyway.
Why not me?

Camp Toehold

Sometimes I feel like I'm at Camp Toehold on the edge of Western Civilization. The other day I got my Polar Bear badge for a perfect week of icy early morning dips. Now I'm waiting for my taxes to go down so I can afford to go to Camp again next year.

Conundrum

Silence sacrosanct is scarce.
Sound is almost all encompassing
And angst invading each one's share
Of privacy
Seems to regulate the day.

Dark and quietness combined
Are also rare.
There is a share
Of quarreling too difficult
To bear
By those so finely tuned
That they're aware
Of distant screeching, howling, rumbling
And even faint white noise
Seeming evident
Nearly everywhere.

Egress

My friend is enwombed within a cocoon.
She does not hear my friendly overtures;
Tulips tell her it's too soon to bloom.
This year, in April, they are tightly budded
And fear the cold.
She rebuffs me and I slowly walk away.
Trusting.

Failure Finesse

A try that doesn't succeed
Is nevertheless worth a good cry,
Because the effort invested in the deed
Beguiles the learner to sigh;
Taking inventory of what was discovered,
And suddenly realizing that it mattered
That even though the prize was tattered
And far from first, the illusion was shattered
That effort is wasted unless you are battered
With media blitzes and parades,
While practicing for those elusive accolades.

Grammar

Grammar is not like a whimsical butterfly
Fluttering free without the constraints of basic
    rules
Taught in good schools.
Students assigned to read or write on subjects
    of their own peculiar inventions
Miss out on the good intentions
Of writers like Hemingway, Milton, Socrates and
    Frost
Who have always been bossed
By past masters of self-expression.
Teachers who firmly refuse to release their
    pupils
To the fancies and peccadilloes of their own
    young, tender and uninitiated minds
Are not unkind.
Good English instructors are very stern.

Harbingers

Two bulbs in shallow water in a glass
Begin to sprout.
Daily their promising green stems
Grow visibly,
Tantamount to spring,
And bring
Fresh and unexpected blossoms
Into view;
White narcissus new
In the coldest, darkest season
Of the year;
Winter:
Evolution in a microcosm.

Haste

Time is now torpedoed and telescoped;
Condensed relentlessly.
Aging is out; racing, pacing and
        finishing are in and win
Epaulets for each participant
Who dares to speed upon the parapet
Of vast accomplishment
Without a crumpled sag
In his plump bag
Of tricks.

Information Overload

Extricate the hooks of consternation
Impaling attentiveness and dragging it away
From the order of the day
Because the sense of obligation
To the momentary task
Is split
And doesn't fit.

International Trade

Stimmies* are gimmies;
A short-cut high
To pie in the sky,
A toke, a joke and never mind why,
Just die, and ask questions later
Like who paid, and who stayed
And ate the contents
Of the refrigerator.

*Stimmies: stimulants; drugs.

Jelly Jam

Certain assumptions titillate
And predicate.
Mischievous discussions about nothing
Substantial
Like who ate the last of the strawberry jelly
And forgot to tell someone
To go to the store for more?
(Knowing full well that the dirty rat who did it
Hid it.)

Journeyman

Please jack up my brain
It's been run over by a thought train
And may never regain
The capacity to feel real pain,
Because I left my video headphones
Out in the rain
Again.
Where is Spain?

Kaleidoscope

Spent beauty* in the autumn of the year
Leaves black branches silhouetted
        against a sunrise;
An even trade; a fresh clean palette
        of light to cheer
Our faces
As we say our morning graces.

*Spent beauty: colored leaves.

Kids*

I would prefer silence
But since I can't have it,
I will acquiesce
To the noise,
Especially of the girls and boys.

*For Andy

Mapping*

I'm mapping the days.
Just now sleep takes a large part of them;
Long dozes in the morning;
My thoughts a haze.
Someone said something the other day about a
    maze,
Which, if completed properly
Could lead to the fulfillment of goals
And actually avoid the shoals
Which, if encountered, might obliterate
My aims.
Tomorrow I'll start by getting up
For three nutritious squares,
Turn off the T.V. for awhile,
Find a matching pair of socks,
Take stock
And beckon fresh resolve.

*For depressed people.

Money Scramble

Cultivating sophisticated lifestyles
That constantly need refining
Requires cash
And makes hash
Of our best budget intentions.
It isn't easy
To do without that bright and breezy
Recreational spending
Especially when payday is pending
However we all know what that means:
Beans.
Again.

Omnibus

I'm an audience of one for my thoughts;
Rambunctious profundities abound,
And priorities might just as well cast lots
To determine just which subject shall expound.
Tomorrow I will surely have an answer
To submit upon the delegated day;
My new composure, dashing as a dancer,
Reflected in the contents of my brilliant resume.

Peregrine Point

Reverberating across ravines of conscious
    and unconscious thought
One permeating bramble spikes the notion
    that consistency
In word, intention and attitude
Cannot be bought
But must be sought
Repeatedly.

Prayer

I am prey.
The onslaught is upon me;
The analyst within me has its way;
Reviewing past events,
Rehearsing future ones;
Turning sleepless nights into day.
Shall I take another pill?
No, I've had enough, anyway.
Someday this will all go away,
I pray.

Pretty and Pert*

A paucity of creases on an older face
Might remind the more astute observer
That years of aging minus the comely grace
Of wrinkles
Present a pert but possibly false demeanor
And signify that proof of echelons of
      experience
Has been erased,
Belying the evidence
Presented on an honest calendar.

*For those considering cosmetic surgery.

Princess Plot

She'd bought into everything under the sun
That promised to help her become
A desirable woman;
Oceans of lotions and potions and oils galore.
She put them on, faithfully reading the labels
And dressed to the nines in her silks and her
    sables
Indeed was the toast of the town;
A beauty of great renown
Except that when she began to speak
She forgot to think to seek
Thoughtful, considerate things to say
And all of the glamour that she would portray
Became an illusion betraying her hope
Of becoming a princess
Instead of an ambient trollop.

Pumpkins

Remember the pumpkin patch?
We took the kids out there to pick out pumpkins.
A plethora of pumpkins;
Did somebody come along and pick all of those
      pumpkins
And make pies out of them?
Or perhaps, let them rot
And then turn them into dogfood or catfood?
Would that have been nutritious for the pets?
Nobody knows
Except maybe the jack-o-lantern
And he shows
Nothing.

Quark Quirks*

A twinkle-farque
Glows in the dark.
It hasn't been invented yet,
But they're sure it will become a pet
Which will require rations
In such gross proportions
That we'll have to feed it the national debt
In order to be able to afford to bet
At the twinkle-farque park
Being built now in the dark.

*A political lampoon about taxation; a
boondoogle.

Quintessential Quest

When I lay it upon my bed at night
My head is as hard as a rock.
I glance at the lighted clock
From time to time
And squelch the urge to get up
And do an inconsequential errand.
Finally I win the fight
With insomnia
And slip ever so softly
Into a gentle, untroubled sleep;
My ritual of twists and turns complete;
My psyche, and all of its ruminations
At rest.

Rancor

Rage convoluted upon rinds
Of hopes devoured in a vortex
Of suctioned promises
Has stacked itself in various kinds
Of boxes.
Like foxes
Recipients of these torpid substitutions
Polish righteous elocutions
To deliver in the air
And despair
Of finding someone there to answer back
Except perhaps a tack
On a bulletin board.

Remnants

Each remnant was meticulous;
All sewn into a homemade quilt;
Patterns quite ridiculous;
Arrays of plaid and paisley,
Checks and stripes and plains
And here and there a spray of daisies
On a field of azure blue,
All competing for attention of the eye
Which took its cue
From the brightest hue.

Grandma knew
How to put the pieces back together
From the swatches that she'd saved,
And also knew
How to wipe a tear away
Saying nothing;
Nodding, understanding.

Rx From A Good Psychiatrist:
Cognitive Course Correction*

I'm hoping to correct your thinking now
With a minor maneuver called manipulation;
You put ignominy on vacation
And abbreviate your frown
While I persuade your snoozing rationale
That it's almost always possible
To make sweet lemonade
To trade
For sour lemons
When it is necessary to do so.

*For Dr. George Christian Harris

Salient Shadows*

We cross each other's paths from time to time
And faint familiar flickers of recognition
Flash across our faces and we keep a scurrying
        line
Preventing us from meeting face to face
To share ambitions
Or perhaps a warm embrace
Because we've studied burying the memories we
        share
And become so good at it we barely seem to
        care
Whether or not the other one is even there.

*This is a sad little poem.

Saturday Football Fan*

Having eclipsed our earlier arrogance
Carved from budding and brashly abundant
   confidence
The pinnacle of total success seemed imminently
   achievable
But sadly wasn't retrievable
From the morass of underestimated obstacles
And unexpectedly unleashed tactics
Of talent from the other side;
We cried
And went home.

*For Coach Jim Sweeney

Stupor*

Help me to sustain
The ability to tolerate the pain;
The stinging, burning, throbbing aching feelings
That reverberate across my weary frame,
Sending migratory notice to my brain,
Saying what a shame;
Another hour, day or week
Down the drain.

*For those who suffer from chronic pain.

Swinging*

Sitting on a wooden swingseat
Pumping up to meet the sky
Blue and clouds and branches meet
In a milieu telling why
There isn't an answer for everything;
Just as there are days like this,
Sitting on a swinging swing,
The wind brushing down to kiss
Your face reminding you that
Sometimes swinging on a swing
Is exactly
Everything.

*For Julie

Tempo

A sudden freshet sluiced the sullen earth
With quenching rebirth
And once again the intricately ordered labyrinth
Of life clinging to hopeful logarithms
Of time and chance
Stirred
And enhanced the territorial view
With something soft, green and new.

Tolerance

I'm so nice about it while I'm being tortured;
I know I'm just one apple in the orchard
Of civility
And have the sensibility
Not to bother anyone
Just because my head's undone
By something someone did or said.
I've been so darned polite
It's turned off almost all the lights
In my ignition system
And my head
Feels like a dead
Battery.

Trilliums

Pent is the trillium on the forest floor
Sovereign among the plants discovered there.
Protectorates of beauty all the more;
The tow'ring firs allow the light and air,
And trilliums thrive there
Uninterrupted by a shovel
That would make their secret, hidden home
A hovel.

Tryst*

Mental health professionals are sometimes like
    moms;
They're probably not real cons
But they've got to get the job done
And it's not always fun
And without the courts
They'd be virtually sweeping the streets from
    port to port
Trying to get every psychic flea to agree
To hop away from manic heads
And it would take ten trillion feds
To get a consensus like that
And in each office an ethical acrobat
Versed in friendly persuasion
Willing to work nineteen days a week
At turning the other cheek
Would be required
If people weren't sometimes squired
Into care facilities
To share their troubles
And examine their internal
Psychic circuses.

*Sketch of a mental health professional's life.

Tweet Speak

If a bird bath were a cistern
Waiting for a bird to fly down and have a bite,
It might suggest that the bird had found another
    way
To whet his appetite.
Perhaps a thoughtful crumb-tray provider
Had stocked the larder
When the bird was needing nourishment
To give him some encouragement.

Weather

The phenomenon impacting us each day
(Because it's unpredictable in almost every way),
Is the weather.
A repertoire of casual remarks
Somehow binds us all together;
Acknowledging that only God knows the final
          answer.
So we ask one another
Will it be Sunny?
Rainy?
Will there be Sleet? Hail? Wind? or Snow?
Perhaps a Hurricane will assault us
And blow upon our fair terrain.
Sometimes the weatherman says
It's anybody's guess.
He's a humble man.

EPILOGUE

Mental Illness: The Subtle Stigma

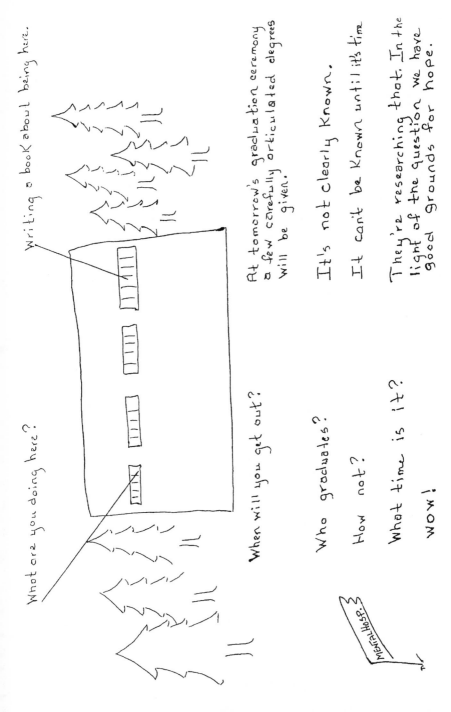

What are you doing here?

Writing a book about being here.

When will you get out?

At tomorrow's graduation ceremony a few carefully articulated degrees will be given.

Who graduates?

It's not clearly known.

How not?

It can't be known until it's time

What time is it?

They're researching that. In the light of the question we have good grounds for hope.

wow!

MENTAL HOSP.

MENTAL ILLNESS:
THE SUBTLE STIGMA

It is not socially acceptable to be mentally ill. I know because I have had numerous episodes of mental illness. Some of them have required confinement in mental hospitals. I have been a patient in seven different treatment facilities for the mentally ill. Two of them were state mental hospitals. My longest stay lasted for eight months. I have known how it feels to hear the door close behind me and to hear the key turn in the lock and to wonder whether or not there would ever be a return to the other side.

I have known how it feels to stand looking out of a window barred to prevent escape and to realize that even if escape were possible there would be nowhere to go. I have known how it feels to lose family, social standing, intellectual and emotional credibility, financial solvency and self-respect. I have known the alienation, despair, bitterness and ruthless cynicism resulting from a diagnosis of mental illness, no matter what particular medical name is attached to that diagnosis. I have known how it feels to fill out a job application and to realize that if there were any indication on it that a mental illness had taken place the job would be automatically denied me.

I have acknowledged my responsibility for my mental illness. And I have known how it feels to wonder whether the embarrassment, the remorse, the shame and the stigma of having been mentally ill will ever go away or whether it is destined to last for an entire lifetime.

For these reasons I have decided to explain not only how it feels to be mentally ill but what can be done about it. It is popular to believe that very little can be done about it. But it has been years now since I have been in any mental hospital and I am becoming more and more confident that there are good reasons for this continuing success not only in staying out of mental hospitals but living a reasonably normal and productive life.

Such a vast body of theory and thought about the care and treatment of the mentally ill has been written and published and studied and implemented that it is somewhat intimidating for the non-professional to venture an opinion. But if it were agreed that any non-professional attempt to solve the enigma is presumptuous and a waste of time we would be ignoring an enormous source of information and help that undoubtedly exists among the mentally ill themselves. We need more bridges between them and society and an understanding of their problems. If we can build these bridges it will help us to know that successful treatment of mental illness most often consists of a cooperative dialogue between the patient and the professional and compassionate understanding by society. It will help to know that if an educated and supportive dialogue can take place publicly it is likely to enlighten all of us and enable us to understand more about the mentally ill and improve their plight.

Strategies, suggestions and optimistic success stories are most likely to be found among people who have confronted, coped, accepted and learned to live with their mental illness.

Where can a definition of mental illness be found? How do you pack all the meanings of the words "crazy", "lunatic", "inmate", "insane" and all of the medical definitions of those words into a single paragraph or a single chapter or even a single book? It's never been done. But do we need to do it in order to have an orderly discussion? Can we make sense talking about something for which there is no general consensus of agreement as to what it is we are talking about?

I suggest that we can make a great deal of sense because we all know that mental illness is a deviation from that common kernel of accord generally acknowledged as goodness, justice, fairness, equality and hope for betterment of our condition. All outrage against social injustice is based on the fact that these commonly held beliefs have been violated. We Americans over the history of our country's establishment and development as a nation have so internalized these basic tenets that we take them for granted as normal and expected conditions.

It is to our credit that our sensitivity to injustice remains intact. Our newspapers report injustice daily. Our court dockets are filled to overflowing with cases waiting to resolve injustices. We have a vast common network of agreement which is so obvious among us, so understood, so present everywhere that it is almost invisible. Yet, we as a nation expect goodness. Mental illness is a contradiction of that basic expectation.

It is the dream gone awry, the hope dashed; the tragic disappointment. It is the nightmare of an assassination or an attempted assassination. It is a brilliant life suddenly interrupted. It is a breadwinner, parent, sweetheart or child removed from a family.

It is often a lonely daily anonymous struggle with torments real and imagined with no one to tell and nowhere to go for help. It is a broken life. It is sometimes sleeping in doorways, under bridges and in dark hallways. It is living with the continuous and indelible knowledge that even though the symptoms have gone away, perhaps even for years, the condition remains and can flare up again at any time. It is constant vigilance in order to be sure that intervention and medical help are sought before institutionalization is required again.

How can it be that we who are able to accomplish so much in the arenas of science, industry, medicine, business, agriculture, commerce and social and political accord cannot crack the riddle of mental illness for all who have it? It will be helpful to understand the answer to that question if we take a brief look at the legacy history has left us.

Michel Foucault, in <u>Madness and Civilization: A History of Insanity In the Age of Reason</u> explains that in the 15th century madmen, as they were then called, were herded onto ships and put out to sea. There were many of them and they became a nuisance to ordinary commerce in the cities. There were no facilities to care for them and their departures upon the waters assured that they would be out of the way. There were no destinations or permanent arrivals for these "ships of fools"; they wandered aimlessly from port to port. The effect of these imposed sojourns was to put the problem out of sight and out of mind. As long as the madmen were going somewhere it somehow seemed like something was being done for them and at the same time solved the moral conflict which might have come about over treating them more or less like cattle.

An additional historical note will help to broaden our perspective. Norman Dain, in his book Concepts of Insanity In the United States 1789–1865 traces the European beginnings: In the 16th and 17th centuries places of treatment; institutions, sanitariums and asylums began to be established for the care of the mentally ill. But these places incorporated into their organizational structures the concept that mental illness was a form of moral depravity. Lessons of moral obligation began to be taught to the mentally ill and a moralizing tone was adopted by all of society. Denunciation of mental illness gradually became the general and accepted version of social criticism. Inability to work; inability to integrate with the group; even extreme poverty were considered not only social but also mental ills in a remarkable blending of moral obligation and civil law.

It is tempting to imagine that we are far removed from these early and crude techniques for handling the problem. But are we? It will help to take a look at a few of the popular misconceptions about the mentally ill in the light of our historical awareness. I will list them and then try to explain why they are misconceptions. These answers cannot be true for everyone but they are likely to be true for many mentally ill people. I have found most of them to be true on occasion.

Misconception #1: Mentally ill people are not intelligent.

Maybe it is assumed that they are not intelligent because if they were they would be able to stop getting ill over and over again. Perhaps some of us conclude they are not smart enough to take charge of their lives and somehow prevent their misfortunes. Why don't they see things for what they are? Actually in a mental illness the understanding of reality is changed so that what seems real to the patient is not matched correctly with what actually is real. This does not necessarily mean that all perceptions are incorrect. In fact, it is quite true that among the many mentally ill there are some of the most literate, sensitive, intelligent, honorable, gentle, insightful, honest and humane persons among us.

Misconception #2: Mentally ill people are all dangerous.

Admittedly, there has been a sensationalizing in the media at times of the vicious, aberrant, uncouth and undesirable actions of some of the mentally ill. It is news-making behavior and there is a certain responsibility to report it to the public. But public opinion does not have the advantage of understanding that the vast majority of the mentally ill do not necessarily commit violent crimes against society and against innocent people. The problem for these less threatening mentally ill people is twofold. Not only are they indeed mentally ill, they are also stigmatized by the actions of their more violent counterparts and held suspect of possible dangerous acts by anyone and everyone who identifies them as a part of the larger group consisting of all mentally ill.

Misconception #3: Mentally ill people refuse to accept the fact that they need to take prescribed medications to help them remain stable.

It is true that good intentions started with the help of prescribing professionals often fall into patterns of denial. Acceptance of medications often equates in the mental patient's mind with owning his or her mental illness, and with it all of the stigmatizing baggage implied. Many mentally ill people, after numerous failures that have befallen them when they have tried to do without their medications have finally realized that the meds are necessary, even though they may have numerous distasteful side-effects like dry mouth, constipation, headaches, drowsiness and temporary disorientation. Finding the appropriate medications requires a dedicated lifelong partnership with the prescribing professional and requires that the patient know his or her medications and what each one is designed to do.

Misconception #4: Mentally ill people are lazy.

Visit a ward in a mental hospital (if you can get permission!). Peek into a room. In many cases you will see clothing dropped on the floor, and an unshaven, sloppy looking person lying on the bed. He or she may indeed appear to be slovenly and unkempt. Depression, one of the most difficult symptoms of mental illness can and often does cause this seemingly lazy behavior. Some patients have to be discharged to short-term living accommodations and soon land on the streets, where they continue to perpetuate the appearance of laziness. Without a good support system of care and rehabilitation these poor souls are doomed to repeat the dreary cycle of re-hospitalization again and again.

There are now more social agencies and churches working to help solve the problems of mentally ill persons. Some have purchased properties; houses that can accommodate small groups or "clusters". In some hospitals when budgets allow, "living skills" are taught to patients who are about to be discharged. These basic skills are for those who have perhaps never had a chance to learn about budgeting, healthful diets and eating habits, grocery shopping and good personal hygiene.

Progress has been made since the days when I first became mentally ill. I am guardedly optimistic that it will continue. Education programs designed to help awareness are gradually beginning to make a difference. I have learned many lessons about myself and have been richly blessed to have had a wide range of experience during my lifetime:

- fortune of good parents
- horse owner at age 8
- Campfire Girl
- 4-H Club member
- high school and college student
- mother
- church member
- Veterans Hospital volunteer
- Home Health Aide caregiver
- Participant in outdoor activities (including childhood summers spent at a rural family beach house, hiking and skiing in the mountains, and bicycling)

Learning does not always take place in schools. It can, and frequently does take place in mental institutions. Bittersweet lessons often last a lifetime. Staff members' continuing devotion to the cause of wellness for their patients is sometimes heroic. These institutions and facilities must be counted in any list of my alma maters.

Residences designed for the care, nurturing and disciplining of discharged and recovering mentally ill persons have been a blessing for me. I have lived in three of them. In these places the staff have coaxed, cajoled and persuaded me to move towards a returning sense of self-worth. They have often been my teachers. Their guidance and encouragement have provided me with new conviction and hope as a former patient returning to society.

In conclusion, poignant words from the poem, "If" by Rudyard Kipling come to mind:

> "If you can fill the unforgiving minute
> With sixty seconds' worth of distance run,
> Yours is the earth and everything that's in it,
> And—which is more—you'll be a man, my son!"

Acknowledgments*

Acknowledgments say thank you
For buttonholes and buttercups
And tender thoughts expressed in
Wordless actions
That knit up factions
Smoothing scowling brows
And turning them into smiles.
Acknowledgments say I remember you
And what you do
Or did for me
And that alone is a soliloquy.

*For Kristin

I have many people to thank for their exceptional compassion and support throughout my sometimes highly challenging life. My parents, Stephen and Hazel Eastman, were compelling examples of unconditional love in their lifelong support and faith in me. My husbands, Jay Tuininga and Ken Nygard, and children Julie, Kristin and Andy have weathered the storms of my numerous illnesses with kindness, love, and understanding. My many medical, psychological and care provider support people have been invaluable and are almost too numerous to mention. Christian Harris, Mary Johnson, Hiram Groshell, Bill Durflinger, Lynette Jeung, Trish Stender, Dr. Harlan White, Dr. Robert Hauk, and Salim Qassis have been especially helpful.

Many friends and church members have helped me more than they will ever know. Some, but not all of them, are Arlett and Olin Nordsletten, Barbara Palecek, Don Firth, Bonnie Thoresen, Don Jensen, Blanche Sylvester, Peter Rice, Signe Bergman, Linda Matthewson Aitken, Jim Peterson, and pastors Shannon Anderson and Verlon Brown. My typist Polly helped me to sustain my writing, even in difficult times; she has been so incessantly correct.

The University of Puget Sound gave me great support while I was there. Arthur Frederick, R. Franklin Thompsen, Hal Simonsen, Bob and Aileen Albertson, and Bruce Rodgers were especially valuable to me.

Finally, my sister Louisa and my brother Hal and his wife Jacque have long been important and compassionate supporters. A special thanks to Hal for helping me to finally get my poems and story into print.

My sincere apologies to those I surely have missed.

Nancy Tuininga

PUBLICATIONS

The following poems have been previously published:

"Failure Finesse," "Salient Shadows," <u>Northwest Views</u>, October, 1990.

"Swinging," "Egress," <u>Other Voices Literary Journal</u>, Fall (premiere) issue, 2003. Reference: Ed. Linda Thompson, Kenmore, WA.

"Mapping," <u>The Good Newsletter</u>, Issue 5. Reference: Steven Collins, Seattle, WA.

"Swinging," <u>The Tidings</u>, Central Lutheran Church newsletter, September, 2003.

"Trilliums," <u>The Tidings</u>, Central Lutheran Church newsletter, October, 2003.

"Money Scramble," <u>The Tidings</u>, Central Lutheran Church newsletter, December, 2003.

"Remnants," "Egress," "Salient Shadows," "Swinging," <u>The Good Newsletter</u>, Issue 6. Reference: Stephen Collins, Seattle, WA.

"Kaleidoscope," <u>The Tidings</u>, Central Lutheran church newsletter, December, 2004. Reference: Pastor Shannon Anderson.

"Tryst," <u>The Good Newsletter</u>, Issue 7. Reference: Stephen Collins, Seattle, WA.

"Money Scramble," <u>The Good Newsletter</u>, Issue 7. Reference: Stephen Collins, Seattle, WA.

"Autobiography," <u>The Good Newsletter</u>, Issue 7. Reference: Stephen Collins, Seattle, WA.

ABOUT THE AUTHOR

Nancy Genevieve Tuininga was born in Seattle, Washington in 1937 and has lived in the Pacific Northwest all of her life. She studied English and philosophy at the University of Washington and the University of Puget Sound in the late '50s and early '60s.

In 1966, while married with two children, Nancy suffered a psychotic break and was diagnosed with bipolar disorder. This resulted in her admission to Harborview Medical Center in Seattle and later to Western State Hospital in Steilacoom, Washington. During subsequent further episodes of mental illness, Nancy was admitted to hospitals in Medical Lake and Spokane, Washington. She was married and divorced several times during this period and started to write poetry sporadically.

In 1989, while recovering and living in an assisted living center in Auburn, Washington, Nancy began to write poems more seriously, finding it valuable to her recovery and a sustaining passion. She began sharing her poems with friends and family who encouraged her to submit her work for publication. She was first published in October 1990 in Northwest Views. Subsequent publications in local newsletters followed.

"Poems from the Attic" is Nancy's first published book.

Made in the USA
San Bernardino, CA
01 February 2018